Computer World

Written by David Orme

Illustrated by Dan Chernett

Published in 2026 by
Norwood House Press
2544 Clinton Street
Buffalo, NY 14224

Printed in the United States of America

Library of Congress Cataloging-in-Publication Data:
Names: Orme, David, author. | Orme, Helen, author. | Chernett, Dan, illustrator. | Mongiovi, Jorge, illustrator.
Title: Computer world / written by David Orme, illustrated by Dan Chernett. The search for life / written by Helen Orme, illustrated by Jorge Mongiovi.
Description: Buffalo, NY : Norwood House Press, 2026. | Series: Phonics all-stars: phase 5c
Identifiers: ISBN 9781978578234 (pbk.) | ISBN 9781978578241 (library bound) | ISBN 9781978578258 (ebook)
Subjects: LCSH: Reading–Phonetic method–Juvenile literature. | English language–Phonetics–Juvenile literature. | Computers–Juvenile fiction. | Outer space–Exploration–Juvenile fiction.
Classification: LCC LB1573.3 O764 2026 | DDC 372.465–dc23

CPSIA compliance information: Batch #CW26NHP: For further i nformation contact Norwood House Press at 1-800-237-9932.

1 The World in a Computer

A pair of experts from another world stared at the screen.

"This is the most powerful computer ever," said Drax. "It holds a complete world in its memory."

The other expert looked on as Drax pressed a button. On the screen, they saw a green and blue planet. There were mountains and forests, and huge cities full of people.

"All those people think they are real. They think they live in a real world," said Drax.

"They don't know that my computer made them all this morning – and filled their heads with fake memories. I even made them like sweet stuff like sugar!"

“What are you going to do with your artificial world?” asked Trex.

“I’m bored with it now. I’ll turn it off this afternoon.”

“But that’s awful! What about all those people?”

“They’re not real! Look, I can control it all!”

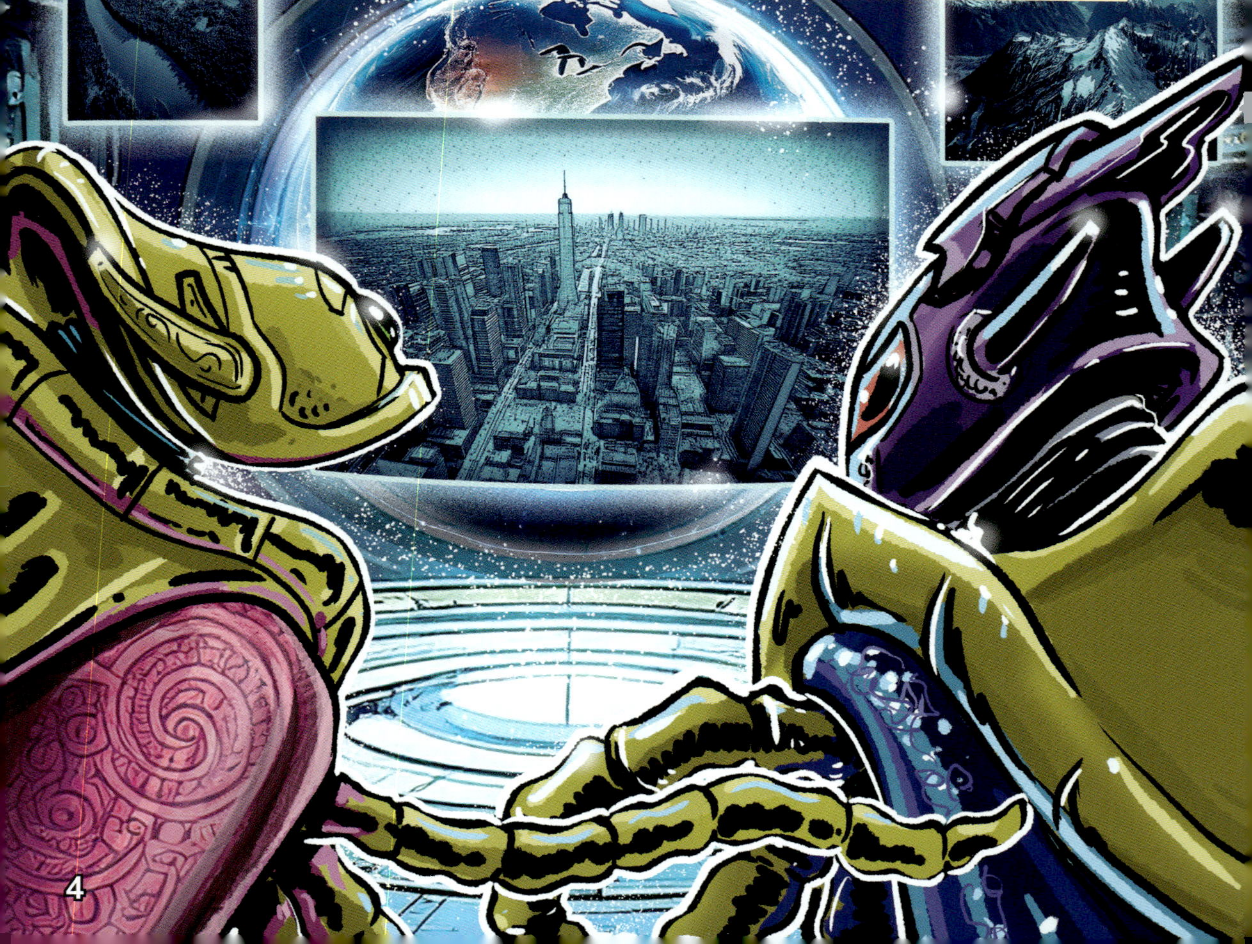

Trex watched in horror as Drax made a huge wall of water crash into a city.

"You have a play if you like," said Drax. "I'm off to make something even better!"

After Drax had left, Trex sat down in front of the screen. These people may be in a computer, but their feelings were real.

He had to save at least one of them!

2 The Creature in the Woods

Hassan Lateef had had a hard day at school. He'd just taken his first exam, and it had been grim. What was worse, he still had a whole week of exams to come!

Now he was plodding through the woods on his way home.

Suddenly, a very odd creature was standing in front of him.

"Hey!" said Hassan. "Love the fancy dress costume."

"I am an expert from another world – the real world," said Trex. "You are just part of a computer program! And it's going to be switched off at five o'clock this afternoon!"

"Ha ha – right," said Hassan nonchalantly. "What's this, a show for some tacky TV station?"

Trex did not argue. He grabbed Hassan's arm.

For Hassan, the world disappeared.

3 The Big Turn-Off

"So, let's get this clear," said Hassan. "My world is just a computer program invented by this Drax guy?"

"That is so. Drax is clever, but so am I. I have made a copy of your body, here in the real world, for you to live in."

"But what about my world?"

"Vanished, I'm afraid. Drax switched it off this afternoon."

"Well, at least that means no exams this week. But what am I going to do in this world? I'm not a clever expert like all of you."

"I don't know. But we'll think of something!"

In a giant glass structure at the top of a mountain, a pair of boffins looked at a screen.

"That's amazing!" said the first boffin. "In the world you made in your computer, someone was so clever that they did the same thing – and made a world of their own!"

"That's right! And another expert rescued someone from that world just in time. Then it was shut down!"

"Shall we rescue someone in the same way?"

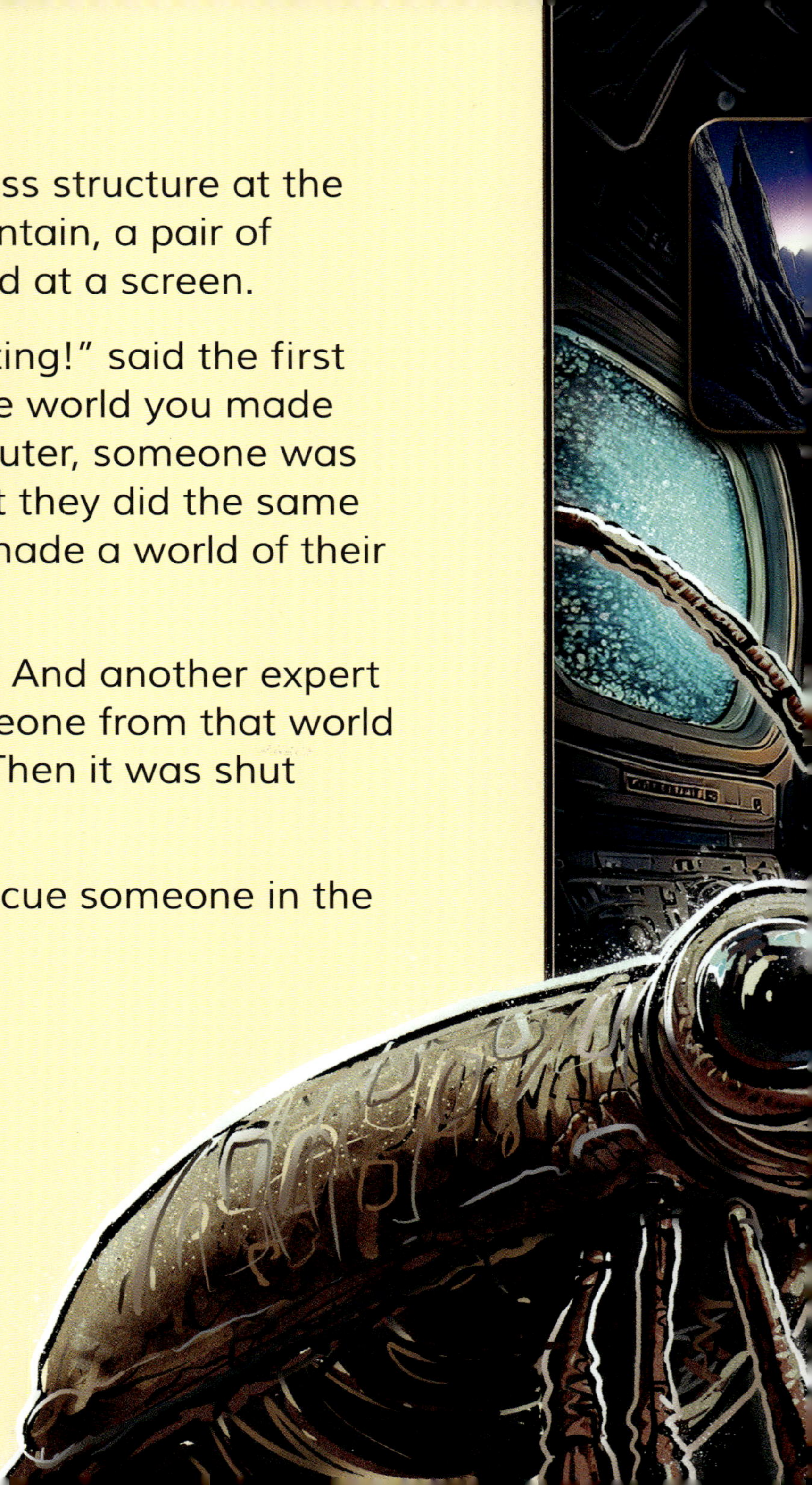

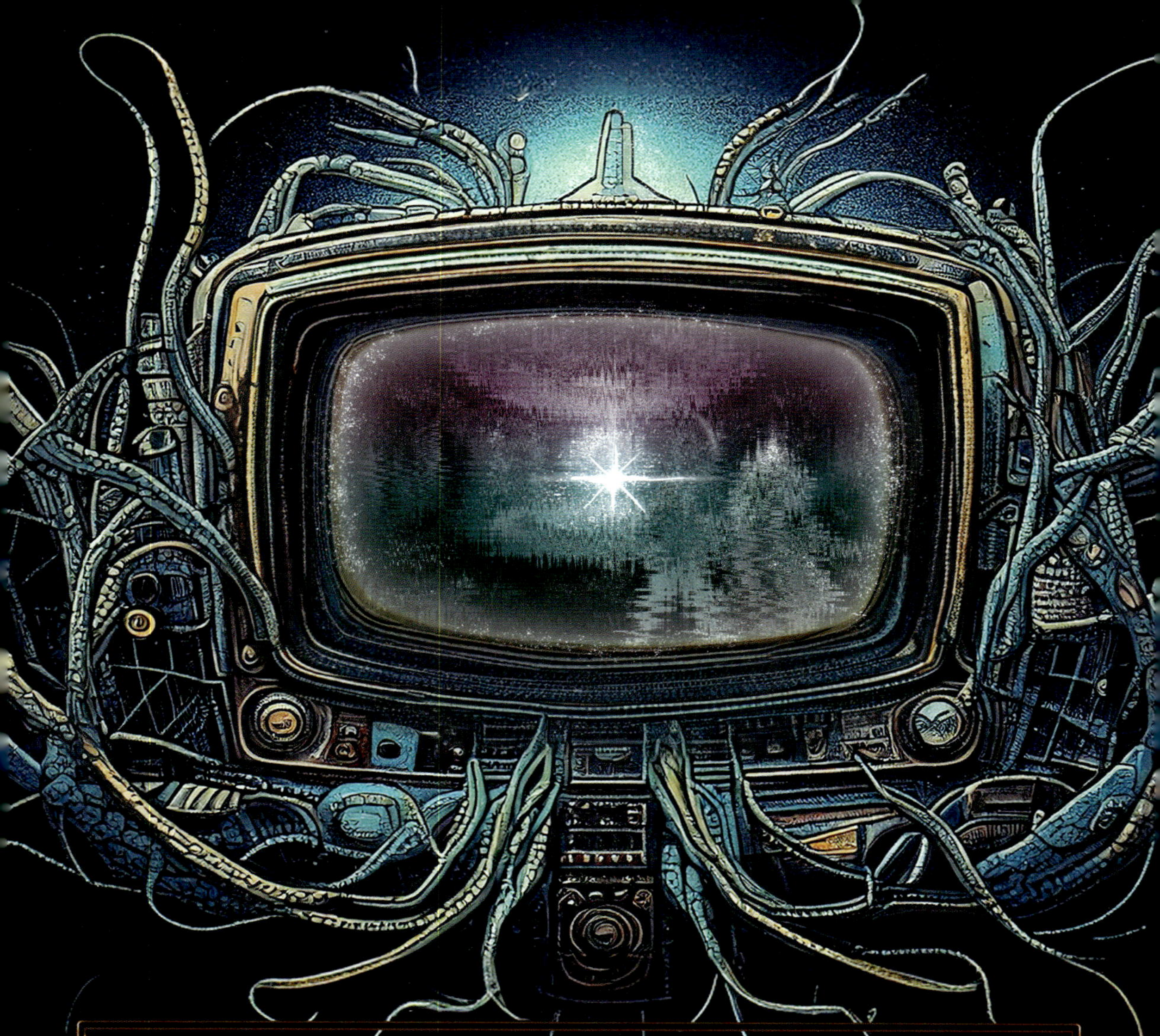

"No, bad idea. As that Hassan boy said, what would they do in our world – the real world?"

With a flick of a switch, the boffin turned off the computer.

The Search for Life

Written by
Helen Orme

Illustrated by
Jorge Mongiovi

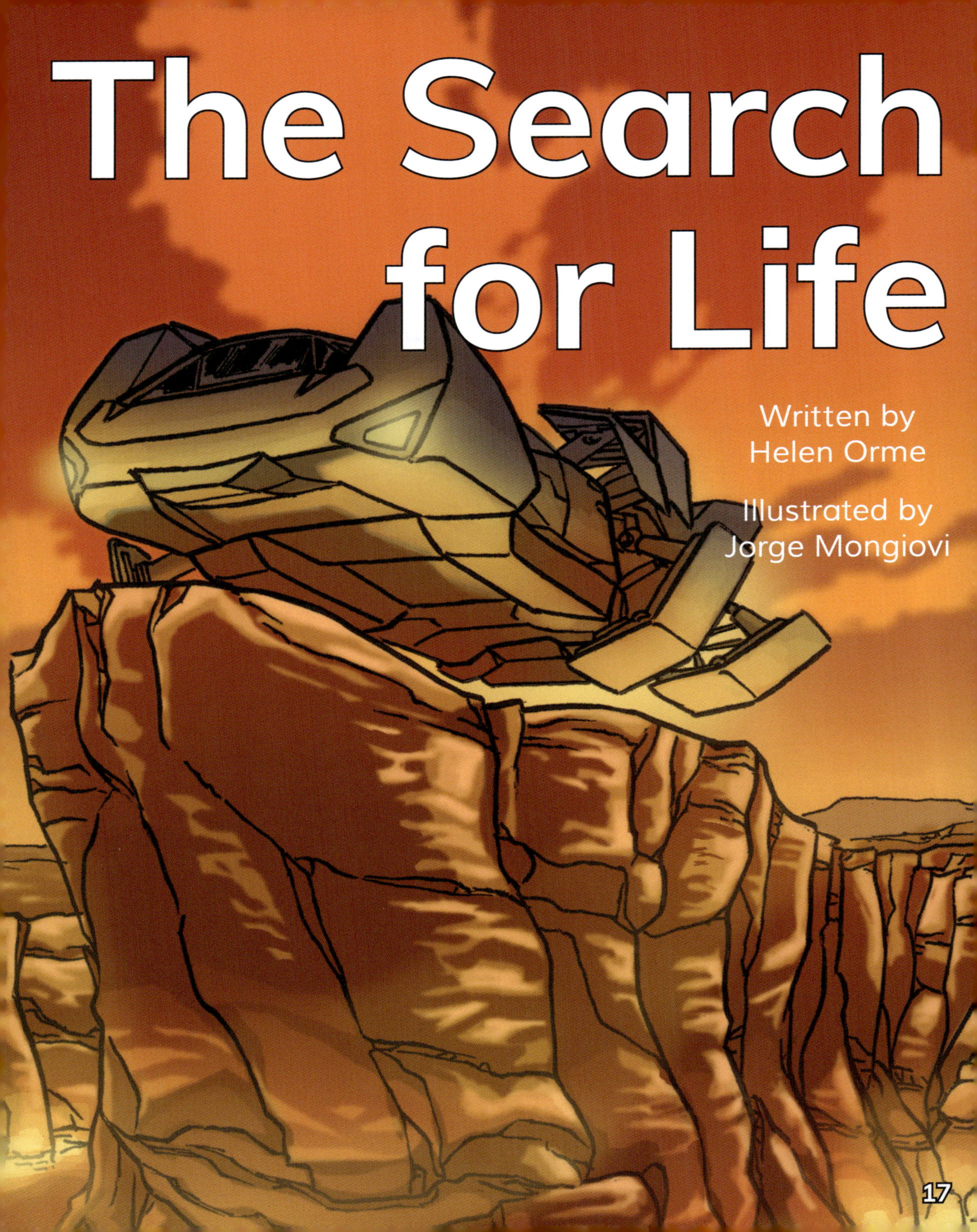

"This star has eight planets," said the science officer. "Let's visit the third one. It's the right distance from the sun for life."

The team of space explorers were searching the galaxy on a mission to find life.

Life was never easy to find. Planets were often too near the sun, too far away, or made of the wrong stuff.

In any galaxy, life was rare.

The planet had a thick atmosphere, without much oxygen.

It didn't look like a place where they would find life, but they decided to land anyway.

The navigator found a safe landing spot. The space ship came to rest on the top of a high cliff.

That was when the problems began.

The ship had four strong landing legs to make it stand level.

Three of the legs hit solid rock, but the fourth landed on uneven ground.

The ship slipped to one side. Part of the ship hit the ground with a crash.

The crew quickly put on their space suits, in case the air leaked out of the ship.

They could all feel the tension in the cockpit.

What if they couldn't take off again? Would they die on this planet, many lightyears from home?

The crew went outside and the engineer checked the ship.

“It’s not too bad,” he said. “It will take time, but we can fix it.”

“Looks like we are going to have plenty of time to explore this planet!” said the science officer. “But I don’t think it is going to be very interesting!”

The space ship had a small aircraft on board.

The navigator and the chief scientist would explore the planet. The rest of the crew stayed behind to help the engineer fix the space ship.

The aircraft took off. The science officer talked to the explorers on the video.

“Take care. With the space ship out of action, we can’t come and rescue you if you get into trouble.”

The sights from the aircraft were amazing. They were near the edge of a great sea.

Huge volcanoes sent up great clouds of smoke and dust. Burning lava poured down into the water, sending up clouds of steam.

Overhead, dark clouds streamed by, pushed on by powerful winds.

"The surface of this planet is just forming," said the science officer. "It's much too early to find life here."

They turned back to the space ship.

The repair work was finished. The ship's cook was clearing up after a meal. The rest of the crew were getting ready for take-off.

The cook looked at all the left-over scraps of food. "No point in taking this into space," he thought. "I'll throw it away."

He put on his space suit and carried the trash out of the airlock. He tipped the scraps out onto the rocks.

There had been no life on the planet.

But there was now.

Countless years later, the planet was a very different place.

The seas were full of life. Forests had spread over the land. Huge cities had sprung up.

A rocket stood ready to blast off into space.

A team of space explorers were ready to search the galaxy for life.